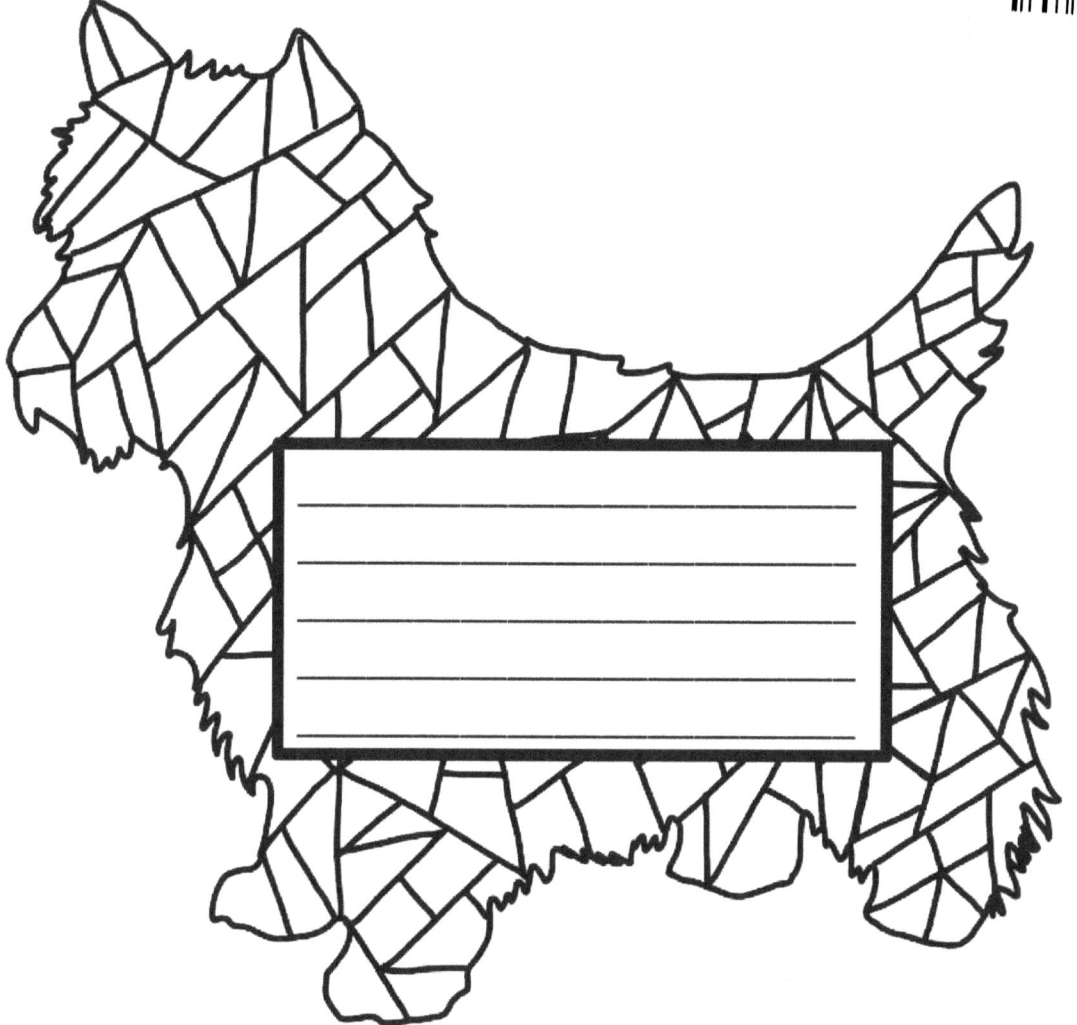

Test Page

Please use this page to try out your
coloring materials and techniques!

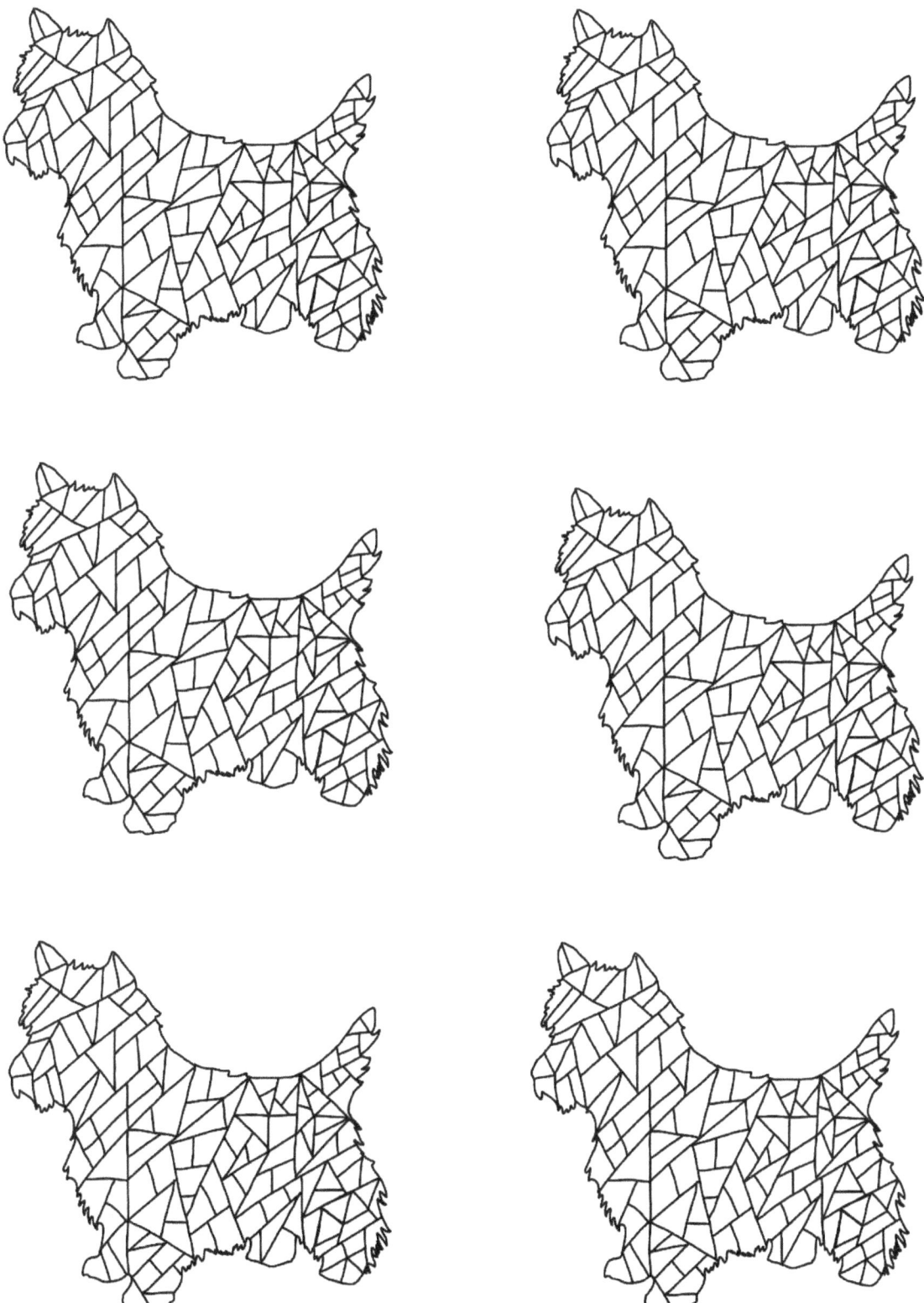

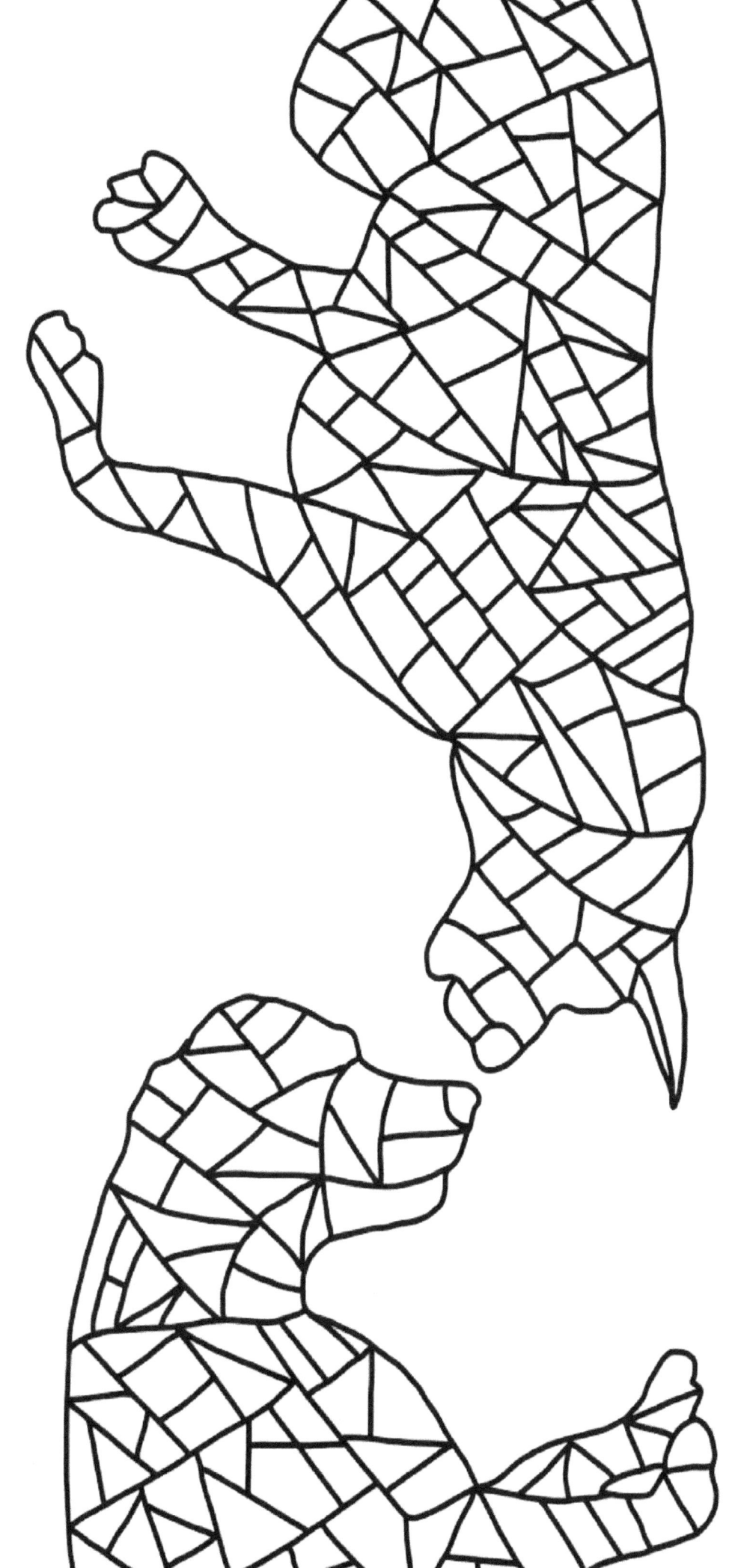

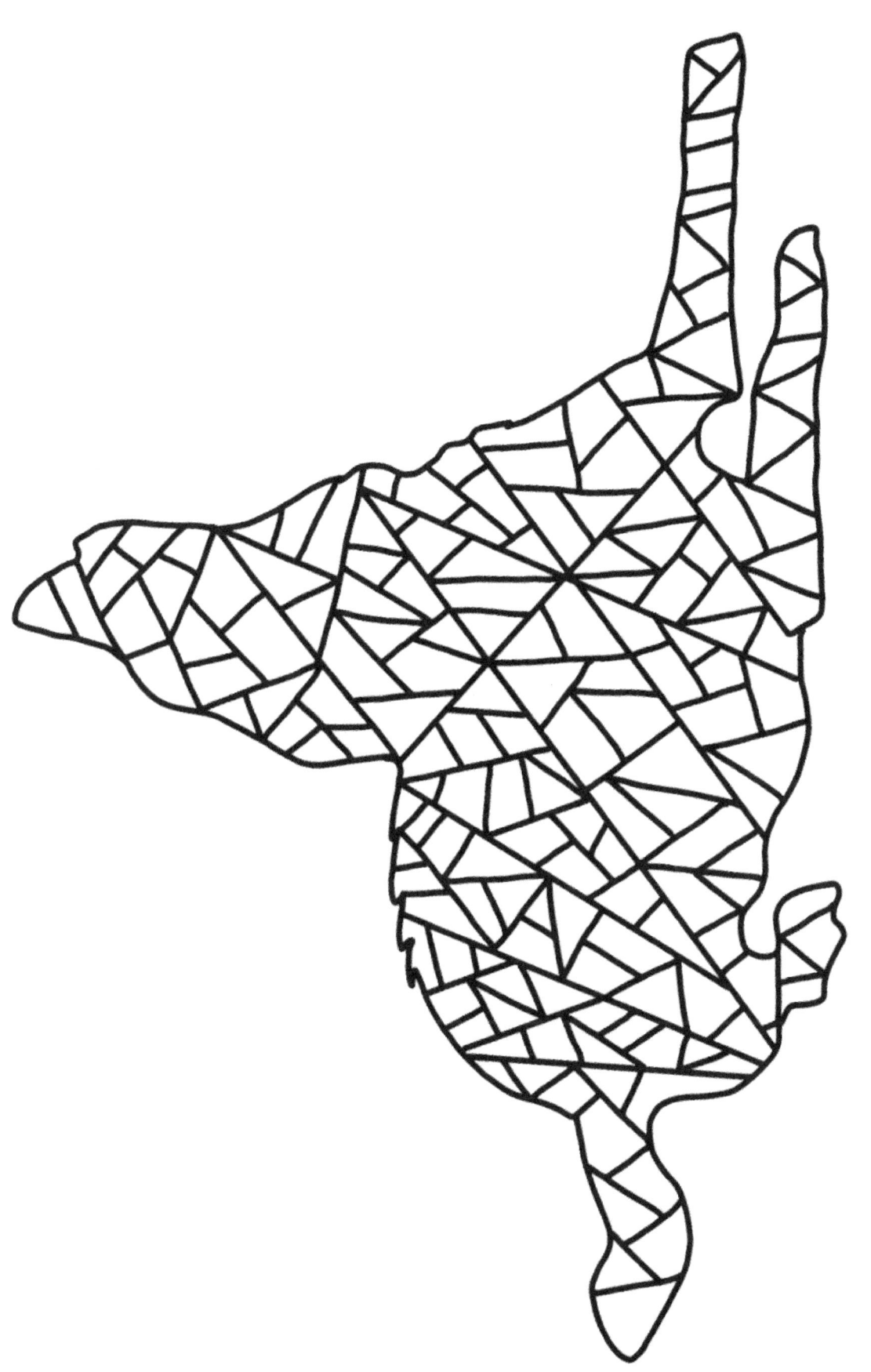

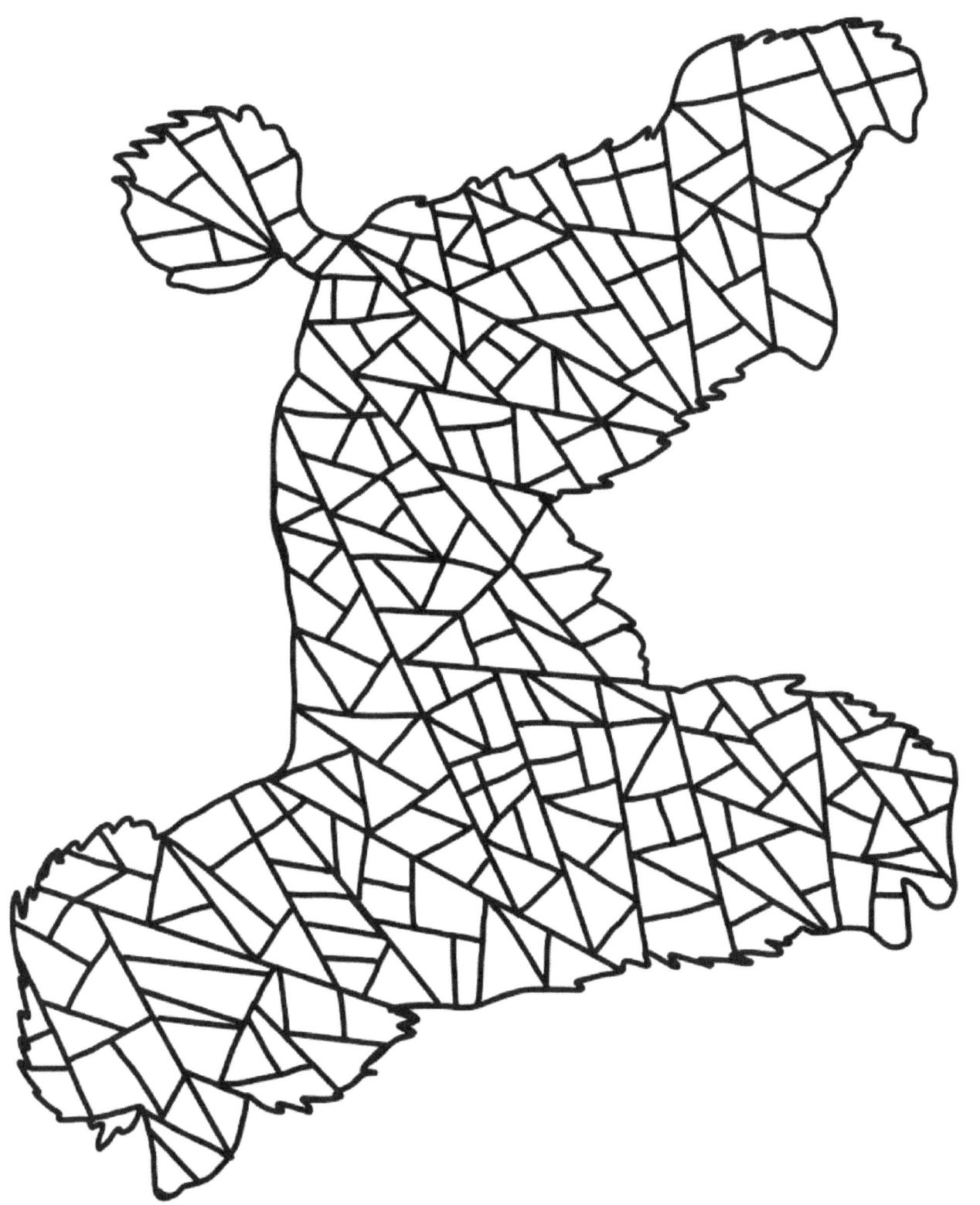

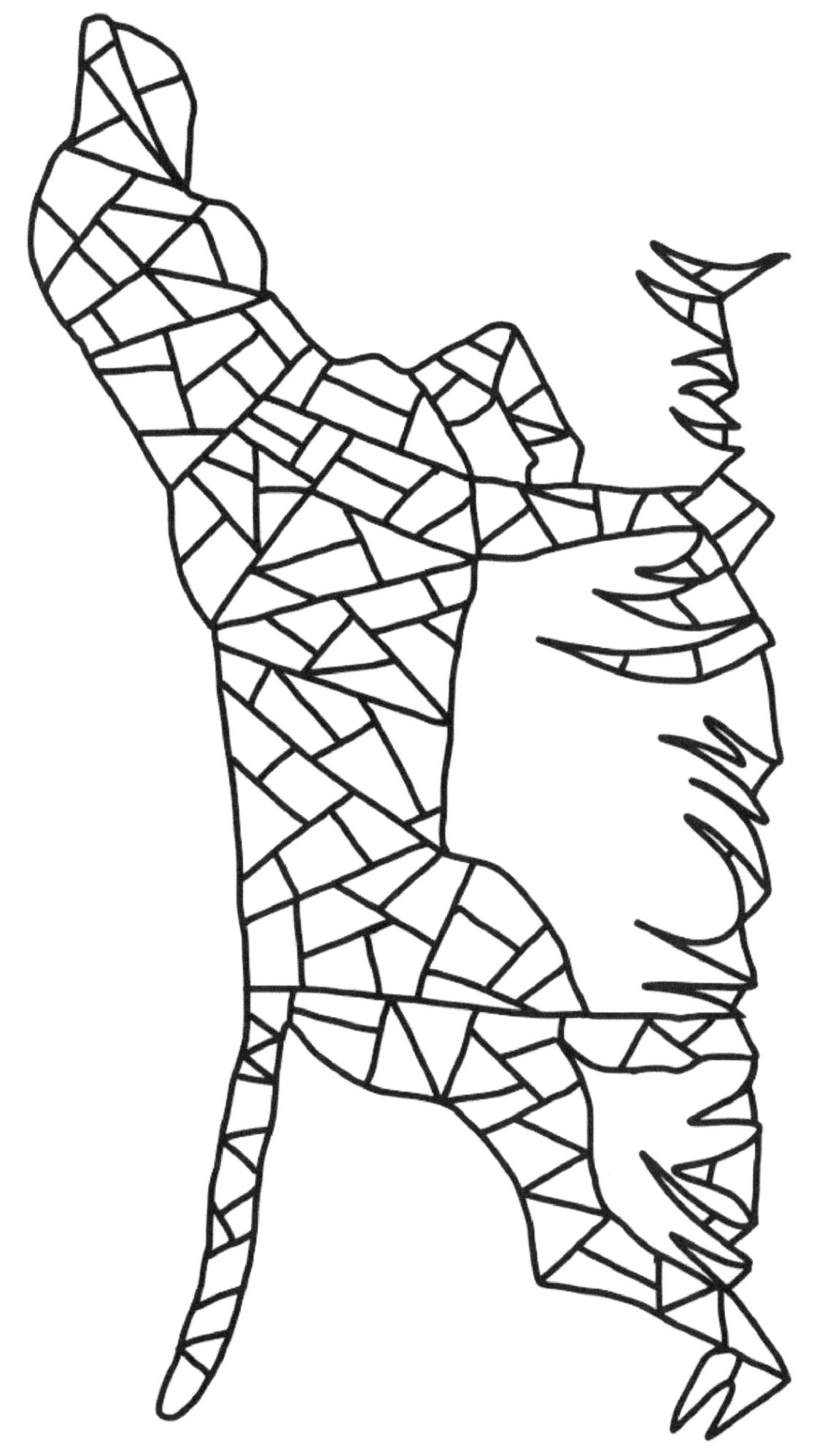

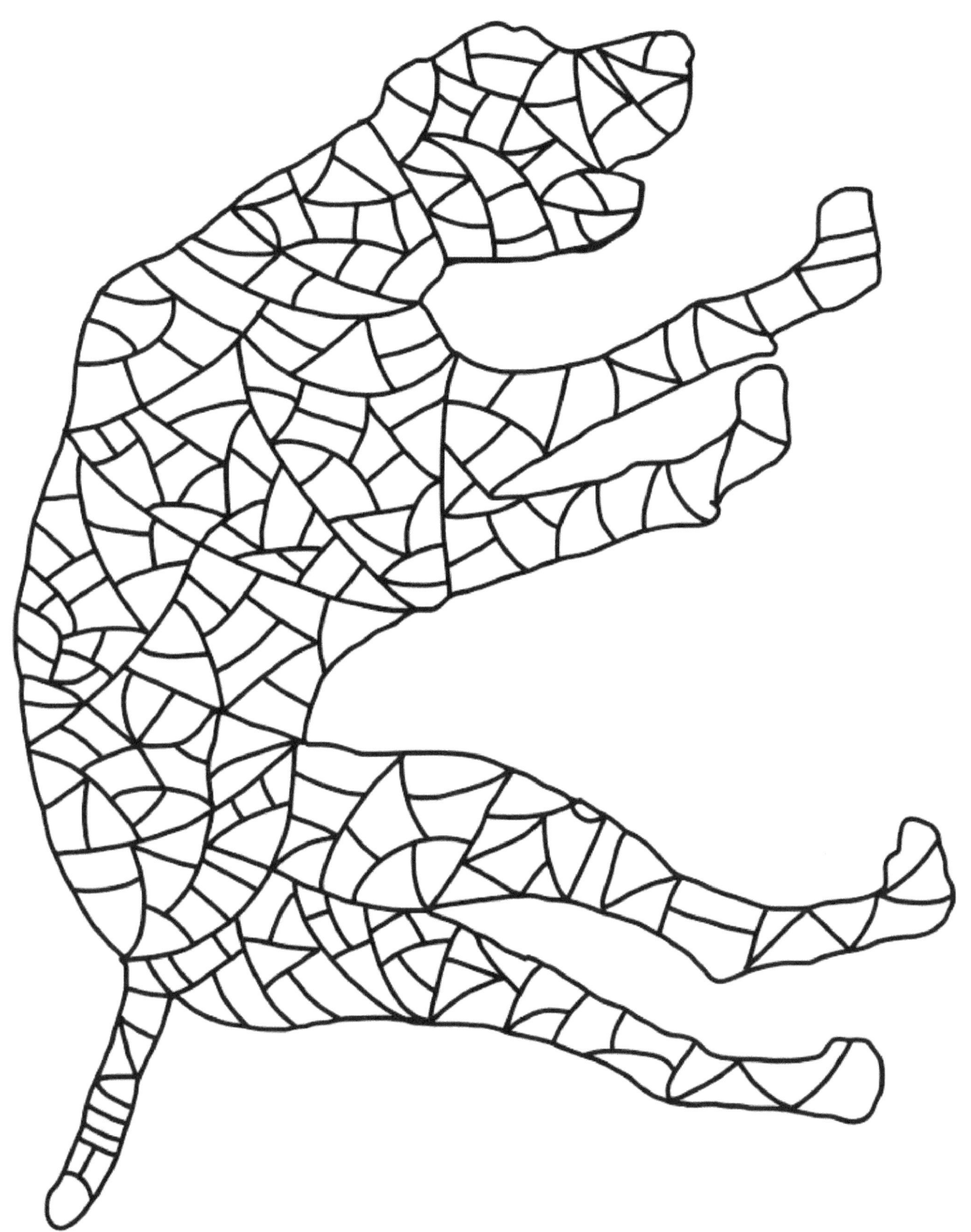

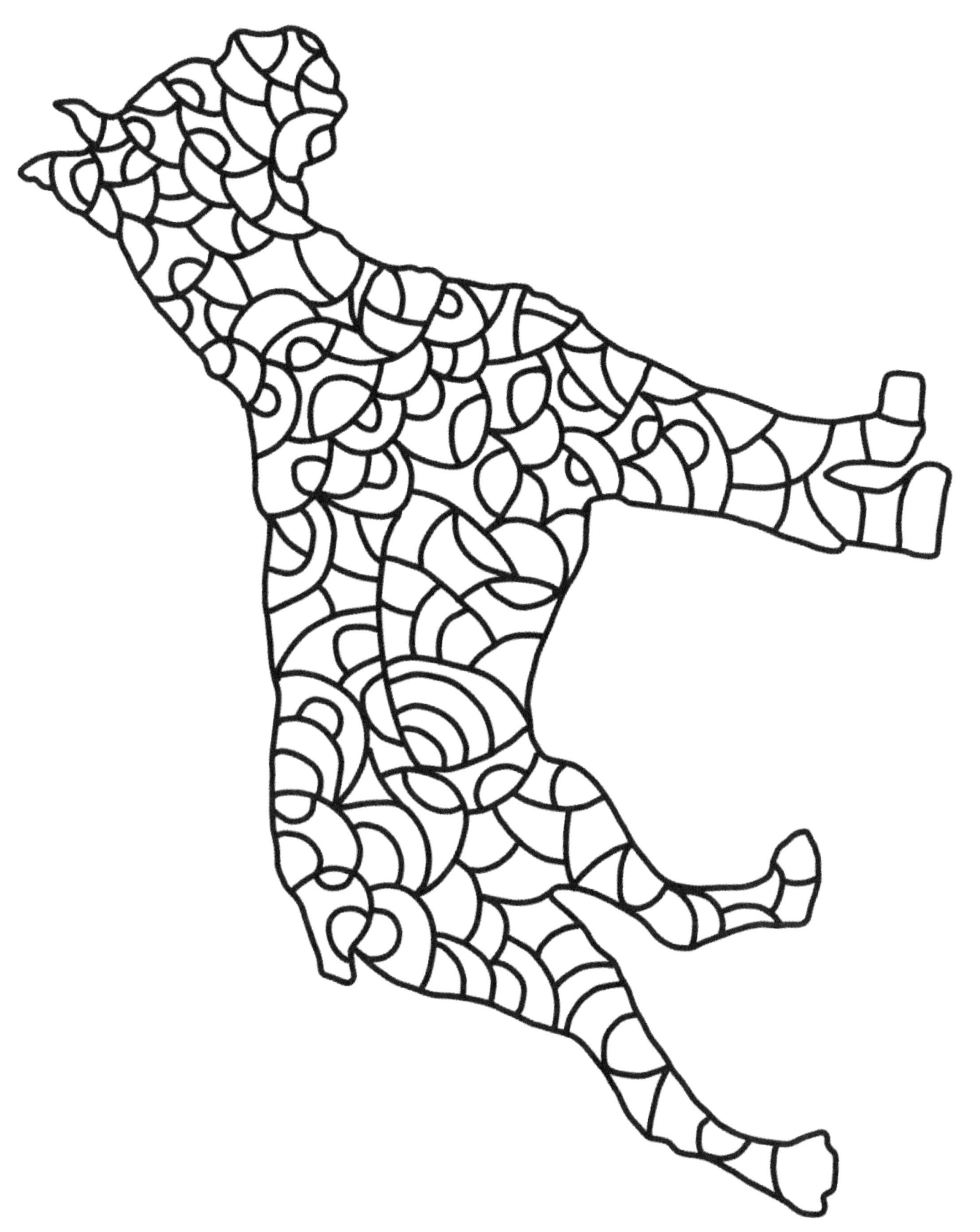

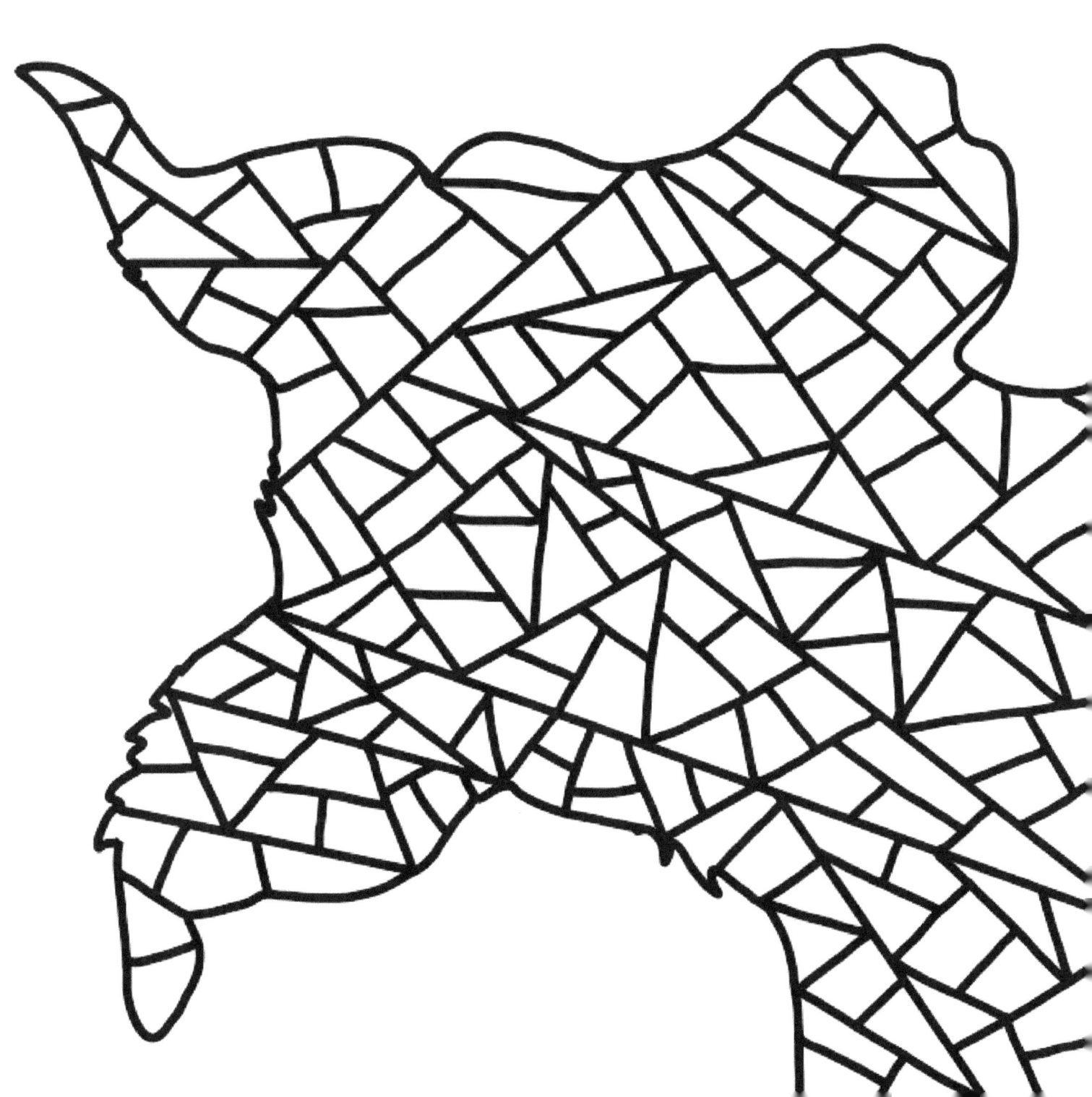

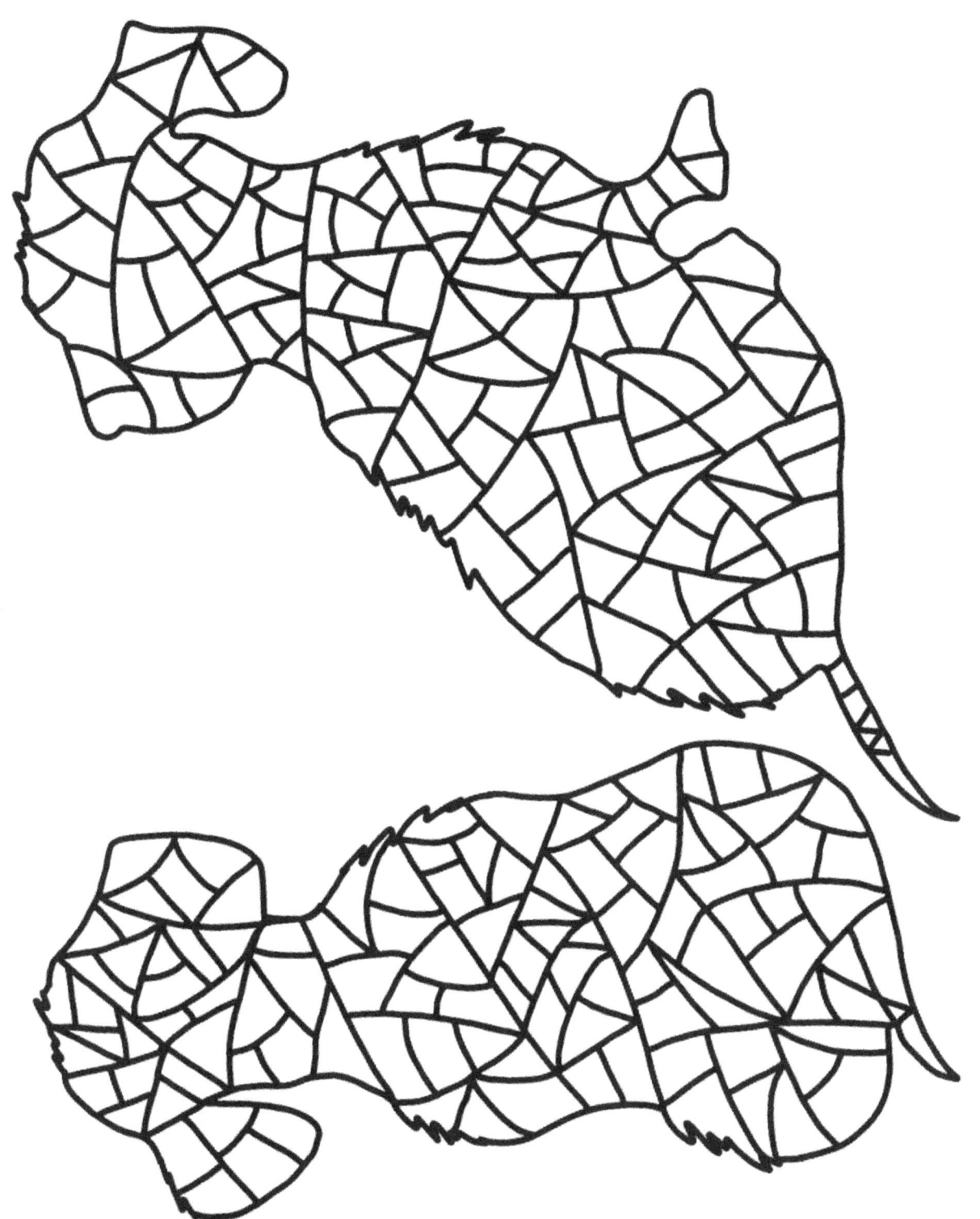

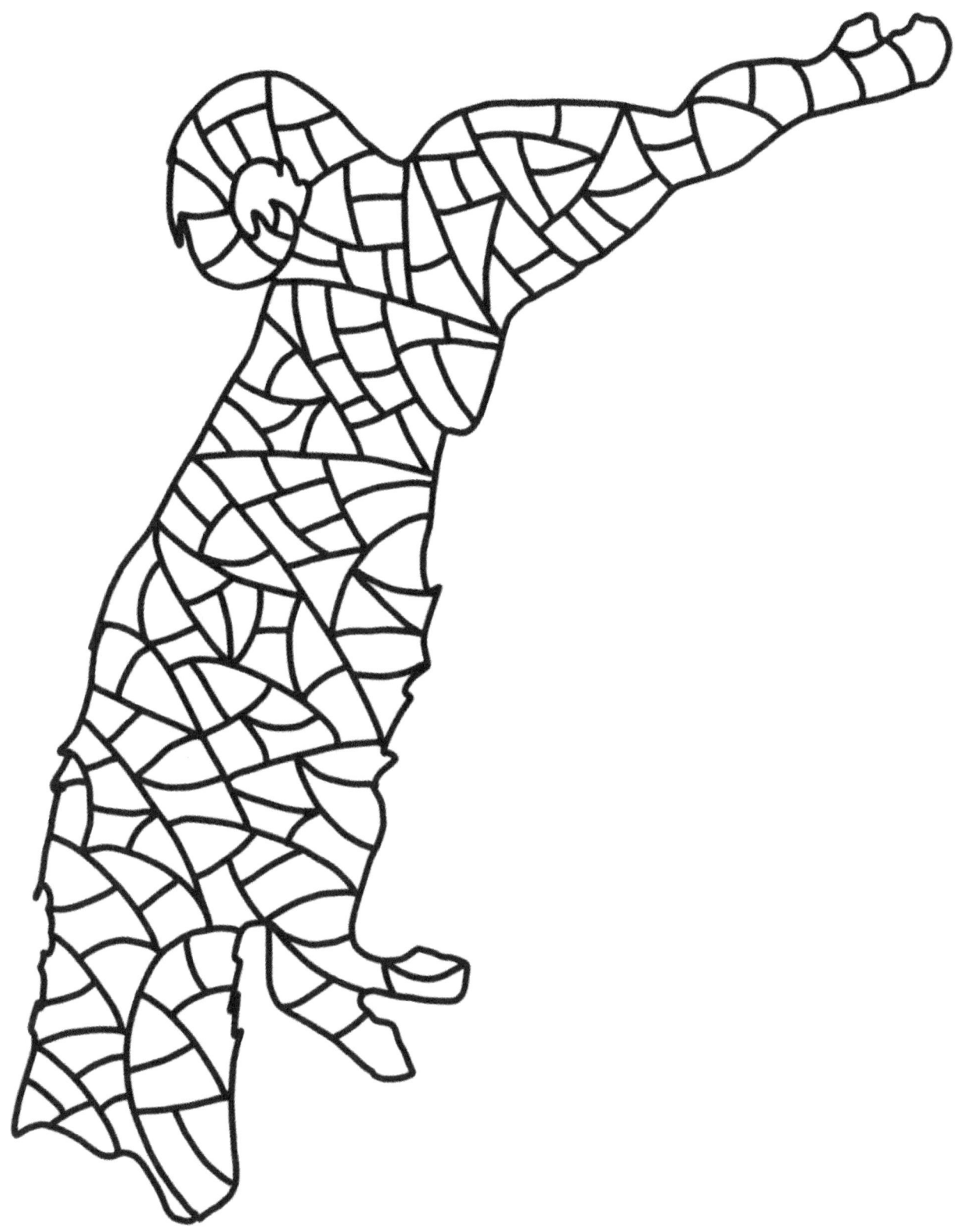

www.ingramcontent.com/pod-product-compliance
Lightning Source LLC
Chambersburg PA
CBHW081856170526
45167CB00007B/3037